L E M O N S

LEMONS
A Book of Recipes

INTRODUCTION BY PEPITA ARIS

LORENZ BOOKS
LONDON • NEW YORK • SYDNEY • BATH

First published by Lorenz Books in 1996

Lorenz Books is an imprint of
Anness Publishing Limited
Boundary Row Studios
1 Boundary Row
London SE1 8HP

This edition distributed in Canada by
Raincoast Books Distribution Limited

Distributed in Australia by Reed Books Australia

ISBN 1 85967 157 8

Publisher Joanna Lorenz
Senior Cookery Editor Linda Fraser
Cookery Editor Anne Hildyard
Designer Lisa Tai
Illustrations Anna Koska
Photographers Karl Adamson, Steve Baxter, James Duncan, John Freeman,
Michelle Garrett and Amanda Heywood
Recipes Alex Barker, Carla Capalbo, Frances Cleary, Carole Clements, Elizabeth Wolf-Cohen, Christine France,
Sarah Gates, Patricia Lousada, Norma MacMillan, Sue Maggs, Katherine Richmond and Laura Washburn
Food for photography Carole Handslip, Wendy Lee, Jane Stevenson and Liz Trigg
Stylists Madeleine Brehaut, Blake Minton and Kirsty Rawlings

Typeset by MC Typeset Ltd, Rochester, Kent
Printed in Singapore by Star Standard Industries Pte. Ltd.

Jacket photography Amanda Heywood

For all recipes, quantities are given in both metric and imperial measures and, where appropriate,
measures are also given in standard cups and spoons. Follow one set, but not a mixture,
because they are not interchangeable.

Contents

$\mathscr{I}$NTRODUCTION

With their distinctive shape and cheerful colour, lemons give us one of life's great flavours. They are one of the truly indispensable kitchen standbys: few other ingredients have lemon's outstanding ability to enhance sweet and savoury dishes. The zest is aptly named; it adds life to all it touches. Finely grated, or in shreds or strips, zest infuses more aroma even than the juice – think of the Italian *gremolata*, zest chopped with parsley and garlic, which gives a kick to any savoury dish.

Lemon juice is indispensable in the kitchen. Freshly squeezed, it has a fragrance that bottled juice can't match. Its tartness is perfect for drinks, from *citron pressé* – fresh juice with water and sugar – to lemonade, barley water and gin sling.

Combined with oil and garlic, lemon juice makes the perfect marinade for meat, fish and vegetables. The acidity is used in marinated raw fish recipes, to give firm texture and turn the flesh opaque. Pick up a lemon whenever you buy fish: they are natural partners. Fried food of all kinds benefits from lemon's acidity, which cuts the grease. Lemon is also a great foil for sweetness and creaminess in all forms: witness lemon curd, mousse and syllabub, to name but a few.

This selection of recipes really shows off the flexibility and range of lemons in cooking. Lemon soups and sauces include Greek *avgolemono* and the classic hollandaise. Several classic and more unusual fish dishes, a Middle Eastern tagine using whole lemon slices, and zingy stir-fries grace the savoury chapters. The final chapter, on cakes and desserts, presents wonderful lemony breads, tarts, biscuits and cakes, as well as sumptuous desserts such as lemon meringue pie and lemon cheesecake.

Lemons are inseparable from the image of the Mediterranean, but they probably came originally from the East Indies. The Romans considered them to be a luxury; when the Roman empire collapsed, lemon cultivation did too. The Moors planted them again in the Sahara, Andalusia and Sicily (still a major supplier) from the eighth century on. Columbus took them to America and it was on long sea voyages that lemons' health-giving properties were first noticed and lemons were given to sailors as protection against scurvy. Now the fruit is enlisted in the fight against cancer and rheumatism. So there are many health-giving and taste-enhancing reasons to make the fullest use of lemons – with the help of these lively and delicious recipe ideas.

Using Lemons

PEELED RIND

This is added to stocks to give a lemon flavour and to counteract any greasy aftertaste. Normally discarded after cooking.

GRATED LEMON RIND

Sometimes called zest, this can be grated finely or coarsely, according to your recipe requirements. Coarsely grated rind can be added to soups, certain savoury dishes and puddings where a lemony flavour is required. It is particularly good added to chicken and duck recipes, in curries and in rich stews, to counteract any greasiness and enhance flavour.

 Finely grated rind similarly adds a delicate, subtle lemon flavour to dishes and is suitable for sauces, cakes, ice creams and sorbets.

WEDGES AND SLICES

Used for garnishing and serving. Lemon wedges tend to be served mainly with fish, rice and other savoury dishes so that extra lemon juice can be squeezed on to the food. Lemon slices can be cut into a variety of pretty shapes and used as decoration for sweet dishes. They are also refreshing added to water or any cool fruit juice or cocktail, and are indispensable in certain alcoholic drinks.

JULIENNE STRIPS

An alternative and pretty decoration for a variety of sweet and savoury dishes.

CANDIED LEMON SLICES

These can be served with meats such as pork or duck, or used in desserts. The slices can be soaked in orange liqueur before adding to desserts. Candied lemon slices are good dipped in chocolate and eaten as a sweet.

DRIED LEMONS

These are used in dried flower arrangements and in pot pourri, where they add a pleasant lemony smell.

Lemon slices

Whole lemons

Whole lemon

Lemon wedges

Lemon wedges

Candied Lemon Slices

Candied lemon peel

Lemon rind

Grated lemon rind

Lemon julienne

PRESERVING LEMONS

LEMON PICKLE

Lemon pickle makes an excellent accompaniment to curries, cold meats and cheese. The chilli powder makes it very hot, so be warned!

Cut eight lemons lengthways into 12 thin wedges. Place in a large sterilized bowl, sprinkle with 50g/2oz/ 4 tbsp coarse sea salt and set aside. Meanwhile, dry fry 15ml/1 tbsp each of fenugreek seeds and mustard seeds for 1–2 minutes until they begin to pop. Place in a mortar or a coffee grinder and grind to a fine powder. Stir in 25–30ml/5–6 tsp chilli powder and 15ml/1 tbsp ground turmeric and sprinkle over the lemons. Add 250ml/8fl oz/1 cup sunflower oil, stir well and then pack into sterilized jars. Close tightly and leave for at least 3 weeks before using. The pickle will keep for 3–4 months.

CANDIED LEMONS

When candying lemons, check their freshness. Make sure the fruit is ripe but firm and the skin is free of blemishes. Always cook and store the rind in large pieces and only cut it as and when you need it. It retains far more moisture this way.

Wash or scrub six lemons thoroughly, cut each in half lengthways and remove the pulp. Simmer the rind in a little water for 1–2 hours until completely tender and drain the liquid into a measuring jug. Make the liquid up to 300ml/½ pint with water, pour into a pan, add 225g/8oz granulated sugar and then simmer over a low heat until dissolved. Bring to the boil, add the rind and then remove from the heat and leave, covered, for 2 days. Drain the syrup into another saucepan and dissolve another 115g/4oz sugar in it. Simmer the rind in the syrup until semi-transparent. Set aside until cool (you can leave it soaking in the syrup for up to 3 weeks). Drain off the syrup and place the rind on a wire rack. Cover and leave to dry for at least

12 hours and then store in screw-topped jars. It will keep for up to 6 months.

CANDIED LEMON JULIENNE

Cut julienne strips from two lemons, blanch in boiling water for 2 minutes and then drain. Gently heat 30ml/2 tbsp water and 25g/1oz sugar, add the lemon julienne and simmer for about 8–10 minutes or until all the water has evaporated and the julienne strips are transparent. Transfer to a plate with a slotted spoon, cool and then store in an airtight container for 2 days before using.

SEAFOOD SALAD WITH LEMON MAYONNAISE

Lemon juice makes a delicious alternative to vinegar in mayonnaise, adding subtle sharpness.

First make the mayonnaise. Place 2 egg yolks in a blender or food processor, add a pinch of salt and 15ml/1 tbsp lemon juice and process briefly to mix. With the mixer running, add 300ml/½ pint/1¼ cups sunflower oil in a slow, steady stream. Add a further 15–30ml/1–2 tbsp lemon juice, process, and then stir in 5ml/1 tsp Dijon mustard. Taste and adjust seasoning, adding more lemon juice if necessary. Arrange pretty salad greens, such as endive, radicchio and lamb's lettuce on four plates. Divide 175–225g/6–8oz fresh white crabmeat and about 225g/8oz cooked peeled prawns among the plates, and top with lemon mayonnaise. Sprinkle with a little paprika and serve. Serves 4.

$\mathscr{B}$ASIC $\mathscr{T}$ECHNIQUES

To grate the rind, use the finest side of a cheese grater, rubbing the fruit firmly, but lightly, up and down the jagged puncture holes, turning the lemon as you go. Make sure that you remove only the yellow outer rind and not the bitter white pith.

Alternatively you can remove rind with a tool known as a zester. Hold the lemon firmly in your left hand and pull the zester towards you. It will remove very fine strands of just the outer rind, leaving the white pith behind. Remove as much rind as required.

To make lemon wedges, to serve with fish or where lemon will be squeezed onto food, always cut the fruit lengthways, cutting first in half, then into quarters, and finally into thin wedges. By this method, juice will be directed downwards when squeezed.

SIMPLE IDEAS

• **Lemon Tea**: remove rind from one lemon using a grater or zester and infuse with a black tea to make a delicious hot or cold drink.

• **Real Lemonade**: remove the rind, using a potato peeler, from three lemons and place in a bowl with 175g/6oz sugar and 900ml/1½ pints/3⅔ cups boiling water. Leave to cool, add the juice of the lemons and strain. Serve well chilled.

• **Lemon Sandwiches**: cut lemons into very thin slices and sandwich between thin, buttered wholemeal bread. Serve with smoked salmon.

For decorative lemon wedges, cut the fruit in half crossways, cut in half again through the stalk or bottom end and then cut into thin or thick wedges as preferred.

TO PEEL COMPLETELY

Cut a slice from the top and the base of the lemon, set the fruit on its base and cut down from the top in thick strips, removing both the rind and the pith. If the lemons are very small, pare away the skin as you would an apple, making sure to remove all the white pith along with the rind.

BUYING AND STORING
LEMONS

- Always buy the largest and freshest lemons you can find.

- Choose fruit that is truly lemon yellow. Butter-yellow lemons may have lost some of their acidity in ripening.

- If possible buy unwaxed fruit, especially if you intend to use the skin.

- Whole lemons will keep fresh in the fridge or a cool place for about two weeks.

- Cut lemons should be wrapped in clear film and used as soon as possible.

- Lemon slices can be frozen.

To make julienne strips, use a canelle knife which will thinly remove the rind in long, unbroken strips. Alternatively, remove the rind with a potato peeler, trim the edges and then cut the pieces of rind into fine, delicate strips.

TO PEEL RIND

For use in stocks, stews, casseroles, or drinks, peel thick strips from the lemon with a potato peeler. This will remove the outer rind without cutting down to the bitter pith.

13

$\mathcal{G}$ARNISHES AND $\mathcal{D}$ECORATIONS

Cut away rind using a potato peeler and then cut into very fine julienne strips. Scatter over caramelized oranges or use to decorate cheesecakes or mousses.

Cut through the peel to the centre of the lemon slice and simply twist to make an S shape. Use to top a savoury pâté or as a garnish for fish or risotto.

Slice the lemon horizontally as thinly as possible, using a very sharp, preferably serrated, stainless steel knife. Remove any pips before using in drinks, or to decorate a cheesecake.

Use a canelle knife to cut vertical strips from the lemon, then cut into thin slices. Use to decorate desserts.

LEMON TIPS

● Lemon juice is a valuable source of Vitamin C; whenever possible, avoid destroying this by adding lemon juice to dishes after they have cooked.

● To extract the maximum amount of juice from a lemon, bring to room temperature and then roll on a work surface for a few minutes before squeezing. Alternatively, microwave for 30 seconds on a high setting, which warms the fruit, yielding more juice.

● Bring out the flavour of mangoes, papayas and guavas by sprinkling with lemon juice.

● Use the pips and juice of a lemon when making jam. Lemon is a good source of pectin, which helps set jam with poor setting properties. The lemon also brings out the flavour of the fruit.

● A few squeezes of juice help poached eggs and boiled rice retain colour.

● A little lemon juice added to water prevents fruit breaking up or losing its shape during stewing.

● A tablespoon of lemon juice will acidulate water sufficiently to prevent vegetables such as sweet potatoes and Jerusalem artichokes from discolouring. Similarly, sprinkle cut avocados, apples and bananas with a little lemon juice to help prevent them discolouring too.

● Refresh your microwave: slice a lemon and float the slices in a bowl of water. Microwave on a high setting for 4–5 minutes. Wipe with a clean cloth.

● Eliminate smells from your fridge, by arranging four or five lemon slices strategically on the shelves and in the door of an empty fridge. Leave for several hours before removing.

● Don't discard squeezed-out fruit. Rub over copper pans and basins with a little salt to make them shine.

Soups and Starters

The lemon's fragrant juice sharpens the flavour

of soups and savoury sauces and perfectly balances the

richness of a smoked salmon starter – just a few drops

make all the difference.

AVGOLEMONO SOUP

This is a Greek soup made with egg, lemon and chicken stock. It is simple to make and has few ingredients, but is full of flavour.

Serves 4

50g/2oz/1 cup thread egg noodles
1 litre/1¾ pints/4 cups hot chicken
  stock
60ml/4 tbsp chopped fresh parsley
30ml/2 tbsp lemon juice
1 egg
4 lemon slices, halved
salt and ground black pepper

COOK'S TIP
After adding the lemon juice and egg mixture, do not allow the soup to boil, or the eggs will curdle. The soup should thicken to a rich, creamy texture.

Place the noodles in a saucepan and add the stock. Bring to the boil and simmer for about 5 minutes or until the noodles are tender.

Add the parsley and stir to mix. Beat the lemon juice and egg together in a bowl and add 30ml/2 tbsp of the hot soup. Pour back into the pan and stir until just thickened. Season, add the lemon slices and serve.

THAI CHICKEN AND CITRUS SOUP

An exotic and aromatic soup that combines delicious flavours from South-East Asia.

Serves 4

15ml/1 tbsp vegetable oil

1 garlic clove, finely chopped

2 boned chicken breasts (about 175g/
* 6oz each), skinned and chopped*

2.5ml/½ tsp ground turmeric

1.5ml/¼ tsp hot chilli powder

75g/3oz creamed coconut

900ml/1½ pints/3¾ cups hot
* chicken stock*

30ml/2 tbsp lemon juice

30ml/2 tbsp crunchy peanut butter

50g/2oz/1 cup thread egg noodles,
* broken into small pieces*

15ml/1 tbsp chopped spring onions

15ml/1 tbsp chopped fresh coriander

salt and ground black pepper

30ml/2 tbsp desiccated coconut and ½
* fresh red chilli, seeded and finely*
* chopped, to garnish*

Heat the oil in a large pan and fry the garlic for 1 minute until lightly golden. Add the chicken, turmeric and chilli powder and stir-fry for a further 3–4 minutes.

Crumble the creamed coconut into the hot chicken stock and stir until dissolved. Pour on to the chicken and add the lemon juice, peanut butter and egg noodles. Stir well, to mix.

Cover the pan and simmer for about 15 minutes. Add the spring onions and fresh coriander, then season well and cook for a further 5 minutes.

Meanwhile, place the coconut and chilli in a small frying pan and heat for 2–3 minutes, stirring frequently, until the coconut is lightly browned.

Serve the soup in bowls sprinkled with the fried coconut and chilli.

ASPARAGUS WITH HOLLANDAISE SAUCE

Hollandaise is a light, buttery, lemon sauce, which is a classic accompaniment to tender asparagus.

Serves 4

675g/1½lb asparagus, trimmed

For the sauce
3 egg yolks
15ml/1 tbsp lemon juice, plus more if
  needed
pinch of cayenne
225g/8oz/1 cup unsalted butter, diced
salt and ground black pepper
finely grated rind of 1 lemon

To make the sauce, combine all the egg yolks, lemon juice, cayenne, and salt and pepper in a heavy saucepan. Whisk together until blended.

Add the butter and set the pan over a medium heat. Whisk constantly to blend in the butter.

When all the butter has been blended into the egg-yolk base, whisk until the sauce just thickens. Add more lemon juice, salt and pepper if needed.

Cook the asparagus, arrange the asparagus on a rack in a steamer over simmering water, cover, and steam until just tender when pierced with the tip of a knife, about 8–12 minutes. Transfer the asparagus to plates and spoon over the hollandaise sauce. Garnish with lemon rind.

POTTED SALMON WITH LEMON AND DILL

This sophisticated starter would be ideal for a dinner party. Preparation is done well in advance, so you can concentrate on the main course.

Serves 6

350g/12oz/1¾ cups cooked salmon,
  skinned and boned
150g/5oz/⅔ cup butter, softened
rind and juice of 1 large lemon
10ml/2 tsp chopped fresh dill
75g/3oz/¾ cup flaked almonds,
  roughly chopped
salt and ground black pepper

COOK'S TIP

For a speedy starter, substitute canned salmon or tuna for the fresh, cooked salmon. Remove any skin and bone before processing.

Flake the salmon into a bowl and then place in a blender or food processor together with two thirds of the butter, the lemon rind and juice, half the dill, and salt and pepper, to taste. Blend until quite smooth.

Mix in the flaked almonds. Check for seasoning, add more if necessary, and pack the mixture into small ramekins. If not serving the same day, clarify the remaining butter and pour over each ramekin to make a seal.

Refrigerate before serving. Scatter the other half of the dill over the top of each ramekin and serve with crudités.

21

Fish Dishes

Whether added to marinades, sauces, batters or

savoury butters, or simply sprinkled over grilled or fried

fish, the juice and rind of lemons lend a piquant

and flavour-enhancing freshness.

WHITING FILLETS IN A LEMONY POLENTA CRUST

Polenta is the name given to fine golden cornmeal. Use the quick and easy polenta if you can as it will give a better crunchy coating for the fish.

Serves 4

8 small whiting fillets
finely grated rind of 2 lemons
225g/8oz/2 cups polenta
30ml/2 tbsp olive oil
15ml/1 tbsp butter
salt and ground black pepper
steamed spinach, to serve
toasted pine nuts, 1/2 red onion, finely
   sliced, and 30ml/2 tbsp mixed fresh
   herbs such as parsley, chervil and
   chives, to garnish

Make four small cuts in each whiting fillet, with a sharp knife, to prevent the fish curling up when it is cooked.

Sprinkle the seasoning and half of the lemon rind over the fish.

Mix the polenta with the remaining lemon rind. Press the polenta on to the fillets. Chill for 30 minutes.

Heat the oil and butter in a large frying pan and gently fry the fillets on either side for 3–4 minutes. Serve with steamed spinach and garnish with toasted pine nuts, red onion slices and the mixed fresh herbs.

SEA BASS WITH CITRUS FRUIT

Along the Mediterranean coast, sea bass is called loup de mer; *elsewhere in France it is known as* bar.
Its delicate flavour is complemented by citrus fruits and fruity French olive oil.

Serves 6

1 lemon

1 orange

1 small grapefruit

*1 sea bass (about 1.35kg/3lb), cleaned
  and scaled*

6 fresh basil sprigs

6 fresh dill sprigs

plain flour, for dusting

45ml/3 tbsp French olive oil

4–6 shallots, peeled and halved

60ml/4 tbsp dry white wine

15g/¹/₂oz/1 tbsp butter

salt and ground black pepper

fresh dill, to garnish

With a vegetable peeler, remove the rind from the lemon, orange and grapefruit. Cut into thin julienne strips, cover and set aside. Peel off the white pith from the fruits and, working over a bowl to catch the juices, cut out the segments from the grapefruit and orange and set aside for the garnish. Slice the lemon thickly.

Preheat the oven to 190°C/375°F/Gas 5. Wipe the fish dry inside and out and season the cavity with salt and ground black pepper. Make three diagonal slashes on each side of the fish. Reserve a few basil and dill sprigs for the garnish and fill the cavity with the remaining basil and dill, the lemon slices and half the julienne strips of citrus rind.

Dust the fish lightly with flour. In a roasting tin or flameproof casserole large enough to hold the fish, heat 30ml/2 tbsp of the olive oil over a medium-high heat and cook the fish for about 1 minute until the skin just crisps and browns on one side. Add the shallots.

Place the fish in the oven and bake for about 15 minutes, then carefully turn the fish over and stir the shallots. Drizzle the fish with the remaining oil and bake for a further 10–15 minutes until the flesh is opaque throughout.

Carefully transfer the fish to a heated serving dish and remove and discard the cavity stuffing. Pour off any excess oil and add the wine and 30–45ml/2–3 tbsp of the fruit juices to the pan. Bring to the boil over a high heat, stirring. Stir in the remaining julienne strips of citrus rind and boil for 2–3 minutes, then whisk in the butter.

Spoon the shallots and sauce over the fish. Garnish with the reserved basil and dill, and the reserved grapefruit and orange segments.

GRILLED FRESH SARDINES

Fresh sardines are flavourful and firm-fleshed, and quite different in taste and consistency from those canned in oil. They are excellent simply grilled and served with lemon.

Serves 4–6

1kg/2lb very fresh sardines, gutted and
*   with heads removed*
olive oil, for brushing
salt and ground black pepper
45ml/3 tbsp chopped fresh parsley,
*   to serve*
lemon wedges, to garnish

Preheat the grill. Rinse the sardines in water. Pat dry with kitchen paper. Brush the sardines lightly with olive oil and sprinkle generously with salt and ground black pepper. Place the sardines in one layer on the grill pan. Grill the sardines for about 3–4 minutes.

Turn the sardines over, and cook for 3–4 minutes more, or until the skin begins to brown. Serve immediately, sprinkled with parsley and garnished with lemon wedges.

FRITTO MISTO

A mixture of seafood is dipped into a lemon-flavoured batter and deep-fried, then served simply, with lemon wedges and salt.

Serves 6

vegetable oil, for deep-frying
500g/1¼lb medium-size fresh prawns,
*   shelled and deveined*
500g/1¼lb squid (about 12 medium),
*   cleaned and cut into bite-size pieces*
115g/4oz/1 cup plain flour for dredging
lemon wedges, to serve

For the batter
2 egg whites
30ml/2 tbsp olive oil
15ml/1 tbsp lemon juice
90g/3½oz/scant 1 cup plain flour
10ml/2 tsp bicarbonate of soda
75g/3oz/⅓ cup cornflour
250ml/8fl oz/1 cup water
salt and ground black pepper

Make the batter in a large bowl by beating the egg whites, olive oil and lemon juice together lightly with a wire whisk. Beat in the dry ingredients, season, and whisk until well blended. Beat in the water, a little at a time. Cover the bowl, and allow to stand for 15 minutes.

Heat the oil for deep-frying until a small piece of bread sizzles as soon as it is dropped in (about 185°C/360°F).

Dredge the prawns and squid pieces in the flour, shaking off any excess. Dip them quickly into the batter. Fry in small batches for about 1 minute, stirring with a slotted spoon to keep them from sticking to each other.

Remove and drain on kitchen paper. Sprinkle lightly with salt, and serve hot with lemon wedges.

RED MULLET WITH LEMON AND TOMATO SAUCE

The sweet, rich flavour of red mullet is perfectly balanced in this dish by its tangy sauce.

Serves 4

4 red mullet, about 175–200g/6–7oz
* each*
450g/1lb tomatoes, peeled, or 400g/
* 14oz can plum tomatoes*
60ml/4 tbsp olive oil
60ml/4 tbsp finely chopped fresh
* parsley*
2 garlic cloves, finely chopped
120ml/4fl oz/½ cup dry white wine
4 thin lemon slices, cut in half
salt and ground black pepper

Scale and clean the fish without removing the liver. Wash and pat dry with kitchen paper.

Chop the tomatoes into small pieces. Heat the oil in a saucepan or casserole large enough to hold the fish in one layer. Add the parsley and garlic, and sauté for 1 minute. Stir in the tomatoes and cook over a moderate heat for 15–20 minutes. Season with salt and pepper.

Add the fish to the tomato sauce and cook over a moderate to high heat for 5 minutes. Add the wine and the lemon slices. Bring the sauce back to the boil, and cook for about 5 minutes more. Turn the fish over, and cook for 4–5 minutes more. Remove the fish to a warmed serving platter and keep warm until needed.

Boil the sauce for 3–4 minutes to reduce it slightly. Spoon it over the fish, and serve immediately.

VARIATION
Small sea bass may be
substituted instead of the red
mullet if you prefer.

SALMON WITH LEMON AND HERB BUTTER

Cooking "en papillote" preserves and enhances the flavour of salmon in this simple but delectable recipe.

Serves 4

50g/2oz/4 tbsp butter, softened

finely grated rind of ½ small lemon

15ml/1 tbsp lemon juice

15ml/1 tbsp chopped fresh dill

4 salmon steaks, about 150g/5oz each

2 lemon slices, halved

4 fresh dill sprigs

salt and ground black pepper

COOK'S TIP

*A different selection of fresh
herbs could be used to flavour
the butter – try mint, fennel
fronds, lemon balm, parsley or
oregano instead of the dill.*

Place the butter, lemon rind, lemon juice, chopped dill and seasoning in a small bowl and mix together with a fork until blended.

Spoon the butter on to a piece of greaseproof paper and roll up, smoothing with your hands into a sausage shape. Twist the ends tightly, wrap in clear film and pop in the freezer for 20 minutes, until firm.

Meanwhile, preheat the oven to 190°C/375°F/Gas 5. Cut out four squares of foil big enough to encase the salmon steaks and grease lightly. Place a salmon steak in the centre of each one.

Remove the butter from the freezer and slice into eight rounds. Place two rounds on top of each salmon steak with a halved lemon slice in the centre and a sprig of dill on top. Lift up the edges of the foil and crinkle them together until well sealed.

Lift the parcels on to a baking sheet and bake for about 20 minutes.

Remove from the oven and place the unopened parcels on warmed plates. Open the parcels and slide the contents on to the plates with the juices.

Savoury Dishes

Lemon combines beautifully with poultry, accentuating

its delicate flavour. It is perfect, too, in vegetarian dishes

– especially when used in combination with fresh

and fragrant herbs.

LEMON CHICKEN STIR-FRY

It is essential to prepare all the ingredients before you begin as this dish is cooked in minutes.

Serves 4

4 chicken breasts (about 150g/5oz
*   each), boned and skinned*
15ml/1 tbsp light soy sauce
75ml/5 tbsp cornflour
1 lemon
1 garlic clove, crushed
15ml/1 tbsp caster sugar
30ml/2 tbsp dry sherry
150ml/¼ pint/⅔ cup chicken stock
juice and finely shredded rind of 1
*   lemon*
60ml/4 tbsp olive oil
1 bunch spring onions, sliced
*   diagonally into 1cm/½in pieces*
salt and ground black pepper

Divide each chicken breast into two natural fillets. Place them between two sheets of clear film and flatten to a thickness of 5mm/¼in with a rolling pin. Cut into 2.5cm/1in strips across the fillets. Put the chicken into a bowl with the soy sauce and toss to coat. Toss in 60ml/4 tbsp cornflour.

Have ready the garlic clove, sugar, sherry, stock, lemon juice, lemon rind, and the remaining cornflour blended to a paste with cold water.

Heat the oil in a wok or large frying pan and cook the chicken in batches for 3–4 minutes. Remove and keep warm while frying the rest of the chicken.

Add the spring onions and garlic to the pan and cook for about 2 minutes. Add the remaining ingredients with the chicken and bring to the boil, stirring until thickened and the chicken is evenly covered with sauce. Serve immediately.

33

TAGINE OF CHICKEN

Lemon slices add a decorative and tangy touch to this richly spiced North African dish.

Serves 8

8 chicken legs (thighs and drumsticks)
30ml/2 tbsp olive oil
1 medium onion, finely chopped
2 garlic cloves, crushed
5ml/1 tsp ground turmeric
2.5ml/1/2 tsp ground ginger
2.5ml/1/2 tsp ground cinnamon
450ml/3/4 pint/1 7/8 cups chicken stock
150g/5oz/1 1/4 cups green olives, stoned
1 lemon, sliced
salt and ground black pepper
fresh coriander sprigs, to garnish

For the vegetable couscous
600ml/1 pint/2 1/2 cups chicken stock
450g/1lb couscous
4 courgettes, thickly sliced
2 carrots, thickly sliced
2 small turnips, peeled and cubed
45ml/3 tbsp olive oil
450g/15oz can chick-peas, drained
15ml/1 tbsp chopped fresh coriander

Preheat the oven to 180°C/350°F/Gas 4. Cut the chicken legs into two through the joint.

Heat the oil in a large flameproof casserole and, working in batches, brown the chicken on both sides. Remove and keep warm.

Add the onion and crushed garlic to the flameproof casserole and cook gently until tender. Add the spices and cook for 1 minute. Pour over the stock, bring to the boil, and return the chicken to the casserole. Cover and bake for 45 minutes until tender.

Transfer the chicken to a bowl, cover and keep warm. Remove any fat from the cooking liquid and boil to reduce by one third. Meanwhile, blanch the olives and lemon slices in a pan of boiling water for 2 minutes until the lemon skin is tender. Drain and add to the chicken with the reduced cooking liquid, adjusting the seasoning to taste.

To cook the couscous, bring the stock to the boil in a large pan and sprinkle in the couscous slowly, stirring all the time. Remove from the heat, cover and leave to stand for 5 minutes.

Meanwhile, cook the vegetables, drain and put them into a large bowl. Add the couscous and oil and season. Stir the grains to fluff them up, add the chick-peas and finally the chopped coriander. Spoon on to a large serving plate, cover with the chicken pieces, and spoon over the liquid. Garnish with fresh coriander sprigs.

TURKEY BREASTS WITH LEMON AND SAGE

Lemon and sage combine to give a lively Mediterranean flavour to this dish.

Serves 4

4 turkey cutlets (boneless slices of breast), about 175g/6oz each

15ml/1 tbsp grated lemon rind

15ml/1 tbsp chopped fresh sage, or 5ml/1 tsp dried sage

50ml/2fl oz/¼ cup fresh lemon juice

90ml/6 tbsp vegetable oil

115g/4oz/1 cup fine dry breadcrumbs

salt and ground black pepper

fresh sage leaves and lemon slices, to garnish

Place each cutlet between two sheets of greaseproof paper. With the flat side of a meat mallet, beat until about 5mm/¼in thick, being careful not to split the meat. Remove the greaseproof paper. Sprinkle the cutlets with salt and pepper.

In a small bowl, combine the lemon rind, chopped sage, lemon juice and 30ml/2 tbsp of the oil. Stir well to mix.

Arrange the turkey cutlets, in one layer, in one or two shallow baking dishes. Divide the lemon mixture evenly between the dishes and rub well into the turkey. Leave to marinate for 20 minutes.

Heat the remaining oil in a frying pan. Dredge the turkey breasts in the breadcrumbs, shaking off the excess. Fry until golden brown, about 2 minutes on each side. Serve the turkey breasts immediately, garnished with sage leaves and lemon slices.

VARIATION

For a delicious alternative, substitute fresh tarragon leaves for the sage.

LEMON AND HERB RISOTTO CAKE

This unusual rice dish can be served as a main course with salad, or as a satisfying side dish. It's also good served cold, and packs well for picnics.

Serves 4

1 small leek, thinly sliced
600ml/1 pint/2½ cups chicken stock
225g/8oz/1 cup short grain rice
finely grated rind of 1 lemon
30ml/2 tbsp snipped fresh chives
30ml/2 tbsp chopped fresh parsley
75g/3oz/¾ cup grated mozzarella
  cheese
salt and ground black pepper
parsley and lemon wedges, to garnish

COOK'S TIP
The best type of rice to choose for this recipe is Italian round grain Arborio risotto rice, but if it is not available, you can use pudding rice instead.

Preheat the oven to 200°C/400°F/Gas 6. Lightly oil a 22cm/8½in round, loose-based cake tin.

Cook the leek in a large pan with 45ml/3 tbsp stock, stirring over a moderate heat, to soften. Add the rice and the remaining stock.

Bring to the boil. Cover the pan and simmer gently, stirring occasionally, for about 20 minutes, or until all the liquid is absorbed.

Stir in the lemon rind, herbs, cheese and seasoning. Spoon into the tin, cover with foil and bake the cake for 30–35 minutes or until lightly browned. Turn out and serve in slices, garnished with parsley and lemon wedges.

BULGUR WHEAT SALAD WITH LEMON AND HERBS

Lemon and mint are the predominant flavours in this traditional Middle Eastern salad.

Serves 6

115g/4oz/³/4 cup bulgur wheat, soaked and well drained

225g/8oz/1 cup seeded and diced tomatoes

1 small red onion, chopped

3 spring onions, chopped

50g/2oz parsley, finely chopped

60ml/4 tbsp chopped fresh mint

120ml/4fl oz/¹/2 cup olive or vegetable oil

75ml/5 tbsp lemon juice

salt and ground black pepper

black olives and mint leaves, to garnish

Combine all the ingredients, except the black olives and mint leaves, in a large bowl. Stir to mix the ingredients thoroughly. Taste and adjust the seasoning if necessary. Serve the salad at room temperature, garnished with black olives and mint leaves.

Bakes, Cakes and Desserts

Lemons add a delightful, sharp flavour to sweet dishes.

Their tart taste makes a wonderful contrast – lending

a clean, tangy freshness to crisp biscuits, pies,

tarts and creamy desserts.

LEMON WALNUT BREAD

This tea bread, with a refreshing lemony flavour, is also perfect for a lunch box or as a coffee-time treat.

Makes 1 loaf

115g/4oz/¹/2 cup butter or margarine,
   at room temperature
90g/3¹/2oz/¹/2 cup sugar
2 eggs, at room temperature, separated
grated rind of 2 lemons
30ml/2 tbsp fresh lemon juice
175g/6oz/1¹/2 cups plain flour
10ml/2 tsp baking powder
120ml/4fl oz/¹/2 cup milk
50g/2oz/¹/2 cup walnuts, chopped
pinch of salt

Preheat the oven to 180°C/350°F/Gas 4. Line the bottom and sides of a 1.2 litre/2 pint/5 cup loaf tin with greaseproof paper and grease. Cream the butter or margarine with the sugar until light and fluffy. Beat in the egg yolks. Add the lemon rind and juice and stir until blended. Set aside.

In another bowl, sift together the flour and baking powder, three times. Fold into the butter mixture, alternating with the milk. Fold in the walnuts. Set aside. Beat the egg whites and salt until stiff peaks form. Fold a large dollop of the egg whites into the walnut mixture to lighten it. Fold in the remaining egg whites carefully. Pour the batter into the tin and bake until a cake tester inserted in the centre of the loaf comes out clean, about 45–50 minutes. Stand 5 minutes before unmoulding on to a rack to cool.

LEMON MERINGUE PIE

A classic, popular pie with a piquant filling and golden meringue topping.

Serves 6–8

275g/10oz/1⅓ cups caster sugar

25g/1oz/¼ cup cornflour

pinch of salt

30ml/2 tbsp finely grated lemon rind

120ml/4fl oz/½ cup fresh lemon juice

250ml/8fl oz/1 cup water

3 eggs, separated

40g/1½oz/3 tbsp butter

23cm/9in pastry case

pinch of cream of tartar (if needed)

COOK'S TIP

Egg whites can be beaten to their greatest volume if they are at room temperature rather than cold. A copper bowl and wire balloon whisk are the best tools to use, although a stainless-steel bowl and electric mixer produce very good results. Take care not to over-beat whites (they will look grainy and separate).

Combine 200g/7oz/1 cup sugar, the cornflour, salt and lemon rind in a saucepan. Stir in the lemon juice and water until smoothly blended.

Bring to the boil over medium-high heat, stirring constantly. Simmer until the mixture is thickened, about 1 minute.

Blend in the egg yolks. Cook the mixture over medium-low heat for a further 2 minutes, stirring constantly.

Remove the saucepan from the heat. Add the butter and mix well.

Pour the lemon filling into the pastry case. Spread it evenly and level the surface with a palette knife. Leave to cool completely.

Preheat the oven to 180°C/350°F/Gas 4.

In a scrupulously clean, grease-free bowl, beat the egg whites until they will hold soft peaks. (If not using a copper bowl, add the cream of tartar as soon as the whites are frothy.) Add the remaining sugar and continue beating until the mixture is stiff and glossy.

Spread the meringue evenly over the filling with a palette knife. Take care to seal it to the edges of the pastry case all round.

Bake for 10–15 minutes or until the meringue is just set and lightly golden brown on the surface. Leave to cool before serving.

LEMON SPICE BISCUITS

The crisp biscuits are perfect for most occasions and are delicious served with ice cream.

Makes 50

240g/8½oz/2⅛ cups plain flour

2.5ml/½ tsp salt

10ml/2 tsp ground cinnamon

225g/8oz/1 cup unsalted butter, at
   room temperature

200g/7oz/1 cup sugar

2 eggs

5ml/1 tsp vanilla essence

grated rind of 1 lemon

In a bowl, sift together the flour, salt, and cinnamon. Set aside. Cream the butter and sugar and beat until the mixture is light and fluffy. Beat together the eggs and vanilla, then gradually stir into the butter mixture with the lemon rind. Stir in the flour mixture. Divide the dough into four parts, then roll each into 5cm/2in diameter logs. Wrap in foil and chill until firm. Preheat the oven to 190°C/375°F/Gas 5. Grease two baking sheets. Cut the dough into 5mm/¼in slices. Place the rounds on the sheets and bake until lightly coloured, for about 10 minutes. Transfer to a wire rack to cool.

LEMON AND RASPBERRY SANDWICH BISCUITS

Crispy lemon biscuits contrast well with their sweet raspberry filling.

Makes 32

175g/6oz/³/4 cup butter, at room
*   temperature*
115g/4oz/¹/2 cup caster sugar
grated rind of 1 lemon
5ml/1 tsp vanilla essence
175g/6oz/1¹/2 cups ground almonds
175g/6oz/1¹/2 cups plain flour
1 egg white, whisked
30g/1oz/¹/4 cup flaked almonds,
*   chopped*
250ml/8fl oz/1 cup raspberry jam
15ml/1 tbsp fresh lemon juice

Cream the butter and sugar then stir in the lemon rind and vanilla. Add the ground almonds and flour and mix together. Wrap and chill. Preheat the oven to 160°C/325°F/Gas 3. Line two baking sheets with greaseproof paper. On a floured surface, roll out the dough to a thickness of 3mm/¹/8in. With a biscuit cutter, stamp out circles. Using a smaller cutter, stamp out the centres from half the circles. Place the rings and circles on the prepared sheets. Brush the biscuit rings with egg white, then sprinkle with the flaked almonds. Bake for 12–15 minutes. Cool, then transfer to a rack. In a saucepan, melt the jam with the lemon juice, brush over the circles and sandwich together with the rings.

LEMON COCONUT LAYER CAKE

This delightful layered cake has a tangy lemon custard filling and a light lemony icing, contrasting with the crunchy coconut topping.

Serves 8–10
115g/4oz/1 cup flour
pinch of salt
8 eggs
350g/12oz/1¾ cups granulated sugar
15ml/1 tbsp grated orange rind
grated rind of 2 lemons
juice of 1 lemon
40g/1½oz/½ cup shredded coconut
30ml/2 tbsp cornflour
250ml/8fl oz/1 cup water
75g/3oz/6 tbsp butter

For the icing
*115g/4oz/½ cup unsalted butter, at
  room temperature*
150g/5oz/1 cup icing sugar
grated rind of 1 lemon
*90ml/6 tbsp fresh lemon juice, plus
  more if needed*
400g/14oz shredded coconut

Preheat the oven to 180°C/350°F/Gas 4. Line three 20cm/8in round cake tins with greaseproof paper and grease. In a large bowl, sift together the flour and salt and set aside.

Place six of the eggs in a large heatproof bowl set over hot water. With an electric mixer, beat until frothy. Gradually beat in 150g/5oz/¾ cup of the sugar until the mixture doubles in volume, for about 10 minutes.

Remove the bowl from the hot water. Fold in the orange rind and half of the grated lemon rind. Gently stir in 15ml/1 tbsp of the lemon juice. Fold in the coconut. Sift over the flour mixture in three batches, folding in after each addition. Divide the mixture among the prepared tins.

Bake until the cakes pull away from the sides of the tin, 25–30 minutes. Leave to stand for 3–5 minutes, then unmould and transfer to a wire rack.

In a bowl, blend the cornflour with a little cold water to dissolve. Whisk in the remaining eggs just until blended. Set aside.

In a saucepan, combine the remaining lemon rind and juice, the water, remaining sugar, and butter. Over a moderate heat, bring the mixture to the boil. Whisk in the eggs and cornflour, and return to the boil. Whisk until thick, for about 5 minutes. Remove from the heat. Cover with greaseproof paper to stop a skin forming and set aside. For the icing, cream the butter and icing sugar until smooth. Stir in the lemon rind and enough lemon juice to obtain a thick, spreadable consistency.

Sandwich the three cake layers with the lemon custard mixture. Spread the icing over the top and sides. Cover the cake all over with the shredded coconut, pressing it in gently.

LEMON ALMOND TART

This classic tart is fresh-tasting, with a crisp, sweet pastry case.

Serves 8

225g/8oz shortcrust pastry
75g/3oz/¾ cup blanched almonds
115g/4oz/½ cup sugar
2 eggs
grated rind and juice of 1½ lemons
115g/4oz/½ cup butter, melted
strips of lemon rind, to decorate

Roll out the pastry to about 3mm/⅛in thick and transfer to a 23cm/9in pie tin. Trim the edge. Prick the base all over with a fork and chill for at least 20 minutes. Preheat the oven to 200°C/400°F/Gas 6. Line the tart base with crumpled greaseproof paper and fill with pie weights. Bake for 12 minutes. Remove the paper and weights and continue baking until golden, about 6–8 minutes. Reduce the oven temperature to 180°C/350°F/Gas 4. Grind the almonds finely with 15ml/1 tbsp of the sugar in a food processor, blender, or grinder. Set a mixing bowl over a pan of hot water. Add the eggs and the remaining sugar, and beat until the mixture is very thick. Stir in the lemon rind and juice, butter, and ground almonds.

Pour into the pastry case. Bake until the filling is golden and set, for about 35 minutes. Decorate with lemon rind.

CHOCOLATE LEMON TART

The contrasting tastes of sweet chocolate and tart lemons complement each other in this delicious tart.

Serves 8–10

250g/9oz/1¼ cups granulated sugar

6 eggs

grated rind of 2 lemons

150ml/¼ pint/⅔ cup fresh lemon juice

150ml/¼ pint/⅔ cup whipping cream

chocolate curls, to decorate

For the pastry case

150g/5oz/1¼ cups flour

30ml/2 tbsp unsweetened cocoa powder

60ml/4 tbsp icing sugar

2.5ml/½ tsp salt

115g/4oz/½ cup butter or margarine

15ml/1 tbsp water

Grease a 25cm/10in pie tin. For the pastry case, sift the flour, cocoa powder, icing sugar, and salt into a bowl. Set aside.

Melt the butter and water over a low heat. Pour over the flour mixture and stir with a wooden spoon until the dough is smooth and the flour has absorbed all the liquid. Press the dough evenly over the base and sides of the prepared pie tin. Chill the pastry case while preparing the filling.

Place a baking sheet in the oven and preheat to 190°C/375°F/Gas 5. Whisk the sugar and eggs until the sugar is dissolved. Add the lemon rind and juice and mix well. Add the cream. Add more lemon juice or sugar if needed. It should taste tart but also sweet. Pour the filling into the pastry case and bake on the hot sheet until the filling is set, for 20–25 minutes. Cool, then sprinkle with the chocolate curls.

BANANA AND LEMON CAKE

Deliciously sweet, ripe banana makes a perfect partner for tart lemon in this heavenly light cake.

Serves 8–10

250g/9oz/2¼ cups plain flour

6.5ml/1¼ tsp baking powder

pinch of salt

115g/4oz/½ cup butter, at room
temperature

200g/7oz/1 cup caster sugar

90g/3½oz/½ cup soft light brown
sugar

2 eggs

2.5ml/½ tsp grated lemon rind

225g/8oz/1 cup mashed, ripe bananas

5ml/1 tsp vanilla essence

50ml/2fl oz/¼ cup milk

75g/3oz/¾ cup chopped walnuts

For the icing

115g/4oz/½ cup butter, at room
temperature

450g/1lb/4½ cups icing sugar

5ml/1 tsp grated lemon rind

45–75ml/3–5 tbsp fresh lemon juice

lemon rind curls, to decorate

Preheat the oven to 180°C/350°F/Gas 4. Grease two 23cm/9in round cake tins, and line the base of each with greased greaseproof paper.

Sift the flour, baking powder and salt into a bowl.

Beat the butter and sugars in a large mixing bowl, until light and fluffy. Beat in the eggs, one at a time, then stir in the lemon rind.

Mix the mashed bananas with the vanilla and milk in a small bowl. Stir this, in batches, into the creamed butter mixture, alternating with the sifted flour. Stir lightly until just blended. Fold in the walnuts.

Divide the mixture between the cake tins and spread evenly. Bake for 30–35 minutes, until a skewer inserted in the centre comes out clean. Leave to stand for 5 minutes before turning out on to a wire rack. Peel off the greaseproof paper.

To make the icing, cream the butter until smooth, then gradually beat in the icing sugar. Stir in the lemon rind and enough of the lemon juice to make a spreadable consistency.

Place one of the cakes on a serving plate. Spread over one-third of the icing, then top with the second cake. Spread the remaining icing evenly over the top and sides of the cake. Decorate with lemon rind curls.

WARM LEMON AND SYRUP CAKE

After soaking in a tangy lemon syrup, this cake is both delightfully sweet and tart.

Serves 8

3 eggs

175g/6oz/3/4 cup butter, softened

175g/6oz/3/4 cup caster sugar

175g/6oz/1 1/2 cups self-raising flour

50g/2oz/1/2 cup ground almonds

1.5ml/1/4 tsp freshly grated nutmeg

*50g/2oz candied lemon peel, finely
  chopped*

grated rind of 1 lemon

30ml/2 tbsp lemon juice

poached pears, to serve

For the syrup

175g/6oz/3/4 cup caster sugar

juice of 3 lemons

Preheat the oven to 180°C/350°F/Gas 4. Grease and line the base of a deep, round 20cm/8in cake tin.

Place all the cake ingredients in a large bowl and beat well for 2–3 minutes, until light and fluffy.

Tip the mixture into the prepared tin, spread level and bake for 1 hour, or until golden and firm to the touch.

Meanwhile, make the syrup. Put the sugar, lemon juice and 75ml/5 tbsp water in a pan. Heat gently, stirring until the sugar has dissolved, then boil, without stirring, for 1–2 minutes.

Turn out the cake on to a plate with a rim. Prick the surface of the cake all over with a fork, then pour over the hot syrup. Leave to soak for about 30 minutes. Serve the cake warm with thin wedges of poached pears.

LEMON PANCAKES

Thin, lacy pancakes, or crêpes, are wonderfully versatile. They are good served very simply with just lemon juice and sugar.

Makes about 12

170g/6oz/1 cup plain flour

10ml/2 tsp caster sugar (for sweet pancakes)

2 eggs

450ml/¾ pint/1⅞ cups milk

about 30g/1oz/2 tbsp melted butter

lemon juice, to serve

sugar, to serve (optional)

PANCAKE-MAKING TIPS

• *Pancake batter should be the consistency of whipping cream. If the batter is at all lumpy, strain it. If it doesn't flow smoothly to make a thin pancake, add more liquid.*

• *Pancake batter can be made in either a blender or food processor. It must have time to stand before using, to incorporate more air.*

To make the pancake batter, mix together the flour, sugar (for sweet pancakes), eggs and milk. Leave to stand for 20 minutes. Heat a 20cm/8in pancake pan over a moderate heat. The pan is ready when a few drops of water sprinkled on the surface jump and sizzle immediately. Grease the pan lightly with a little melted butter. Pour 45–60ml/3–4 tbsp batter into the pan. Quickly tilt and rotate the pan so the batter spreads out to cover the bottom thinly and evenly; pour out any excess batter.

Cook for 30–45 seconds or until the pancake is set and small holes have appeared. If the cooking seems to be taking too long, increase the heat slightly. Lift the edge of the pancake with a palette knife; the base of the pancake should be lightly brown. Shake the pan vigorously back and forth to loosen the pancake completely, then turn or flip it over. Cook the other side for about 30 seconds. Serve sprinkled with lemon juice and sugar, if using.

LEMON CHEESECAKE ON BRANDY SNAPS

Using ready-made brandy snaps gives a quick and crunchy golden base to this simple and delicious classic lemon cheesecake.

Serves 8

½ × 142g/4¾oz packet lemon jelly

450g/1lb/2 cups low-fat cream cheese

10ml/2 tsp lemon rind

75–115g/3–4oz/about ½ cup caster sugar

few drops vanilla essence

150ml/¼ pint/⅔ cup Greek-style yogurt

8 brandy snaps

mint leaves and icing sugar, to decorate

Dissolve the jelly in 45–60ml/3–4 tbsp boiling water in a heatproof measuring jug and, when clear, add sufficient cold water to make up to 150ml/¼ pint/⅔ cup. Chill until beginning to thicken. Line a 450g/1lb loaf tin with clear film.

Cream the cheese with the lemon rind, sugar and vanilla and beat until light and smooth. Then fold in the thickening lemon jelly and the yogurt. Spoon into the prepared tin and chill until set. Preheat the oven to 160°C/325°F/Gas 3.

Place two or three brandy snaps at a time on a baking sheet. Place in the oven for no longer than 1 minute, until soft enough to unroll and flatten out completely. Leave on a cold plate or tray to harden again. Repeat with the remaining brandy snaps.

To serve, turn the cheesecake out on to a board with the help of the clear film. Cut into eight slices and place one slice on each brandy snap base. Decorate with mint leaves and sprinkle with icing sugar.

COOK'S TIP

If you don't have any brandy snaps to hand, you could serve this cheesecake on thin slices of moist ginger cake, or on other thin, crisp biscuits.

MINT AND LEMON SORBET

This sorbet has a very refreshing, delicate taste, perfect for a hot afternoon.

Serves 6–8

450g/1lb/2 cups sugar

475ml/16fl oz/2 cups water

6 mint sprigs, plus more to decorate

6 lemon balm leaves

250ml/8fl oz/1 cup dry white wine

30ml/2 tbsp lemon juice

dill sprigs, to decorate

Place the sugar and water in a saucepan with the washed herbs. Bring to the boil. Remove from the heat and add the wine. Cover and cool. Chill for several hours, then add the lemon juice. Freeze in a suitable container. As soon as the mixture begins to freeze, stir it briskly and replace in the freezer. Repeat every 15 minutes for at least 3 hours or until ready to serve.

To make the small ice bowls, pour about 1cm/½in cold, boiled water into small freezer-proof bowls, about 600ml/1 pint/2½ cups in capacity, and arrange some herbs in the water. Place in the freezer. Once this has frozen add a little more water to cover the herbs and freeze.

Place a smaller freezer-proof bowl inside each larger bowl and put a heavy weight inside, such as a metal weight from some scales. Fill between the bowls with more cooled boiled water, float more herbs in this and freeze.

To release the ice bowls, warm the inner bowl with a small amount of very hot water and twist it out. Warm the outer bowl by standing it in very hot water for a few seconds, then tip out the ice bowl. Spoon the sorbet into the ice bowls, decorate with mint and dill sprigs and serve.

COOK'S TIP

Instead of lemon balm leaves,
fresh flowers can be used in the
ice bowl. Small pansies,
marigolds or geraniums would
all be suitable.

LEMON MERINGUE BOMBE WITH MINT CHOCOLATE

This unusual ice cream has quite the most delicious combination of tastes that you can imagine.

Serves 6–8

2 large lemons

150g/5oz/²⁄₃ cup granulated sugar

150ml/¼ pint/²⁄₃ cup whipping cream

600ml/1 pint/2½ cups Greek natural yogurt

2 large meringues, roughly crushed

3 small mint sprigs

225g/8oz good-quality mint chocolate, grated

Remove the rind from the lemons with a vegetable peeler, then squeeze the juice. Place the lemon rind and sugar in a blender or food processor and blend finely. Add the cream, yogurt and lemon juice and process thoroughly. Pour the mixture into a mixing bowl and add the meringues.

Reserve one of the mint sprigs and chop the rest finely. Add to the cream and lemon mixture. Pour into a 1.2 litre/2 pint/5 cup glass pudding bowl and freeze for 4 hours.

When the ice cream has frozen, scoop out the middle and pour in the grated mint chocolate, reserving a little for the garnish. Replace the ice cream to cover the chocolate and refreeze.

To unmould, dip the bowl in very hot water for a few seconds to loosen the ice cream, then invert the bowl over a serving plate. Decorate with grated chocolate and a mint sprig.

COOK'S TIP

If you prefer, use either milk or plain chocolate instead of mint chocolate. To make a richer ice cream, use cream instead of the Greek yogurt.

LEMON AND MINT CUP

The refreshing flavours of lemon and mint in this delicate cup make a wonderful mixture with an intriguing taste.

Serves 1

4 mint sprigs

2.5ml/¹/₂ tsp sugar

crushed ice

2.5ml/¹/₂ tsp lemon juice

30ml/2 tbsp grapefruit juice

125ml/4fl oz/¹/₂ cup chilled tonic water

lemon slices, to decorate

Crush two of the mint sprigs with the sugar and put these into a glass. Fill the glass with crushed ice.

Add the lemon juice, grapefruit juice and tonic water. Stir gently and decorate with the remaining mint sprigs and slices of lemon.

LEMON AND MINT CURD

Home-made lemon curd is infinitely tastier than the commercial variety. The addition of mint gives this version an interesting extra tang. Buy fresh eggs and try to find unwaxed lemons for this lemon curd.

Makes about 1.5kg/3lb
6 fresh mint leaves
900g/2lb/4 cups caster sugar
350g/12oz/1½ cups unsalted butter,
  cut into chunks
rind of 6 lemons, thinly pared, in large
  pieces, and their juice
8 eggs, beaten

Place the mint leaves and sugar in a blender or food processor, and blend until the mint leaves are finely chopped and mixed with the sugar.

Put the mint sugar and all the other ingredients into a large bowl and mix thoroughly together.

Set the bowl over a pan of simmering water. Cook, whisking gently, until all the butter has melted and the sugar has dissolved. Remove the lemon rind.

Continue to cook in this way, stirring frequently, for 35–40 minutes or until the mixture thickens. Pour into sterilized glass jars, filling them up to the rim. Seal with greaseproof paper circles and cellophane lids secured with rubber bands. Add a label and tie short lengths of string around the top of the jars to decorate. This lemon curd should be used within 3 months.

COOK'S TIP
Store the Lemon and Mint Curd in a cool, dark place for about 1 month. Or, store in the fridge for up to 3 months.

INDEX